THIS BOOK

BELONGS TO:

_____

IF YOU ENJOYED THIS BOOK, CHECK OUT OUR OTHER
ACTIVITY BOOKS ON AMAZON

LANGSTON
PUBLICATIONS

CRICKET FACT #1

DID YOU KNOW?

THE FIRST CRICKET BALL WAS MADE OF WOOL. TODAY, THEY ARE MADE FROM MAINLY CORK, YARN AND LEATHER.

1

PLAYER TEAMS

CAN YOU JOIN UP THE PLAYER TO THEIR INTERNATIONAL TEAM?

JOSH HAZLEWOOD	BANGLADESH
BABAR AZAM	ENGLAND
JOE ROOT	AUSTRALIA
SHAKIB AL HASAN	PAKISTAN
RAVINDRA JADEJA	INDIA

CRICKET COLOURING #1

COLOUR IN THE IMAGE TO BRING IT TO LIFE

3

CODE CRACKING

USING THE TABLE BELOW CAN YOU DECODE THE NAMES OF
THESE 2019 WORLD CUP CRICKET TEAMS?

A	B	C	D	E	F	G	H	I	J	K	L	M	N	O	P	Q	R	S	T	U	V	W	X	Y	Z
Q	T	X	V	B	N	E	R	D	O	Z	C	P	H	L	G	U	I	F	K	A	S	Y	M	W	J

FLAKR QNIDXQ

_ _ _ _ _   _ _ _ _ _ _

QNERQHDFKQH

_ _ _ _ _ _ _ _ _ _ _

YBFK DHVDBF

_ _ _ _   _ _ _ _ _ _

QAFKIQCDQ

_ _ _ _ _ _ _ _ _

BEST BATSMEN

HOW MANY OF THESE BATSMEN CAN YOU FIND IN THE WORD SEARCH?

```
T Z W D L R O O T N L B B N P I X
G G S V A H P W E B X D E D T N H
C O A C O O K Q N X L D E C J W N
W F H V L B T K D T M Q Y O O A D
W X Y F A B Q U U T J Y G J N L Q
E F S D R S J Y L M S Q T E S K R
C O A Z A M K S K S N N N A N E Z
L O D E Y Z Y A A G Z D I L G K E
B Q D H F A Y N R K B G J N V Z X
Q P O N T I N G Q B T S V V I U R
V Y S H I R I A I J M X W G Z Y N
D C X O M C G K O H L I B N R K M
S J G I J Q J K A C F D S P B E M
M A B R A D M A N L T K B V E R T
K G F T R Q U R R H L W Q A G O N
Q P V H A J I A N H P I U B T H I
R N R M Y C K Q K P I B S H F O M
```

AZAM	HOBBS	PONTING
BRADMAN	KALLIS	ROOT
COOK	KOHLI	SANGAKKARA
GAVASKAR	LARA	TENDULKAR

CRICKET FACT #2

DID YOU KNOW?

THE LONGEST CRICKET MATCH INVOLVED ENGLAND AGAINST SOUTH AFRICA IN 1939. IT LASTED 14 DAYS AND HAD TO BE DECLARED A DRAW.

BAT DESIGN

DESIGN THE FRONT AND BACK OF YOUR VERY OWN CRICKET BAT. FEEL FREE TO EXPERIMENT WITH DIFFERENT COLOURS

FRONT   BACK

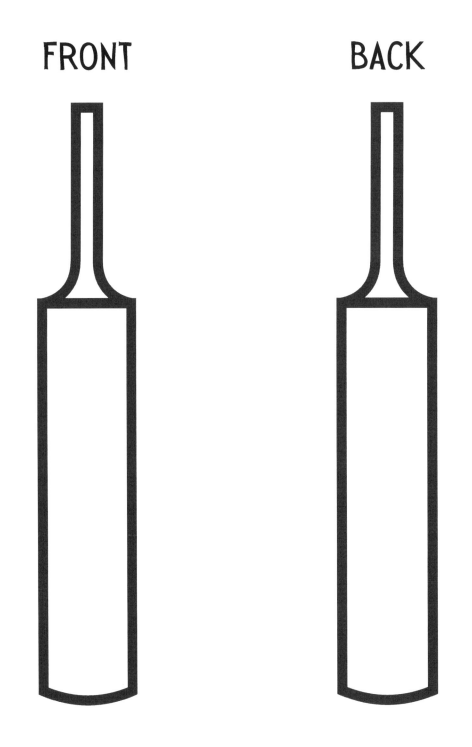

RATE A PLAYER #1

CHOOSE A CRICKET PLAYER AND RATE ALL OF THEIR SKILLS OUT OF 100. WHAT AREAS OF THEIR GAME DO YOU THINK THEY COULD IMPROVE?

PLAYER NAME:

_____

BATTING: /100

BOWLING: /100

THROWING   /100

CATCHING: /100

FIELDING: /100

SPEED: /100

AGILITY: /100

8

CRICKET ADDITION

= 5 = 4 = 2

+ =

_____

+ + 4 =

_____

+ 2 + 3 =

_____

+ + =

_____

+ 2 + =

_____

9

CRICKET FACT #3

DID YOU KNOW?

CRICKET WAS ORIGINALLY
PLAYED WITH TWO STUMPS,
NOT THREE.

CRICKET COLOURING #2

COLOUR IN THE IMAGE TO BRING IT TO LIFE

11

SOLUTION ON PAGE: 94

CRAZY MAZE #1

CAN YOU BOWL THE BALL THROUGH THE MAZE AND INTO THE STUMPS
ON THE OTHER SIDE?

START

MAZE 1

END

12

PLAYER ANAGRAMS

CAN YOU UNSCRAMBLE THESE ANAGRAMS TO WORK OUT WHICH PLAYER
SHOULD BE MADE UP OF THE LETTERS?

FEEDDIR OFLINFFT

_____ _____

RIYCK GTONINP

_____ _____

NMIAR AHKN

_____ ____

KENVI EEPRINSTE

_____ _____

CRICKET FACT #4

DID YOU KNOW?

PAKISTAN BOWLER SHOAIB AKHTAR THREW THE FASTEST EVER BOWL IN 2003 AGAINST ENGLAND, RECORDING A SPEED OF 100.2 MPH.

PERFECT PLAYER #1

BUILD YOUR PERFECT PLAYER BY USING ELEMENTS OF ALL THE BEST
CURRENT CRICKET PLAYERS, E.G. JOE ROOT'S BATTING

BATTING ABILITY: _____

LEFT ARM: _____

RIGHT ARM: _____

SPEED: _____

AGILITY: _____

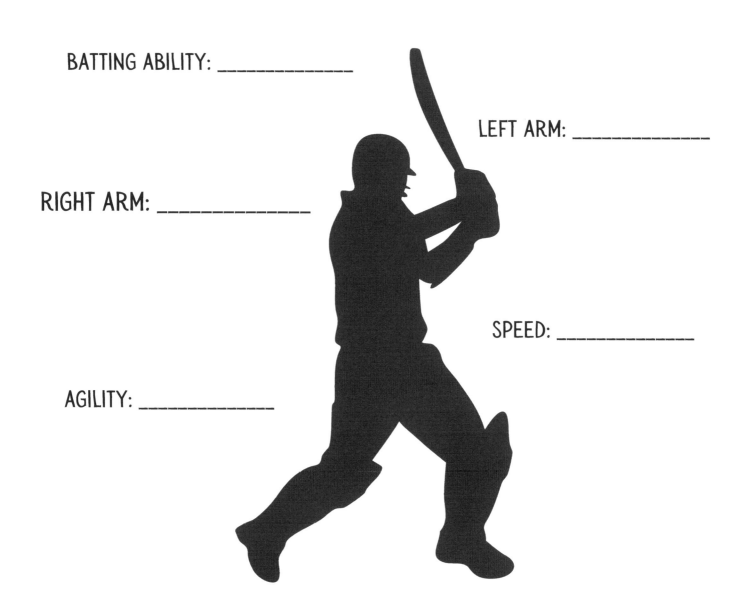

STADIUM LOCATIONS

CAN YOU JOIN UP THE STADIUM TO ITS LOCATION?

THE GABBA	INDIA
EDEN PARK	ENGLAND
KENSINGTON OVAL	AUSTRALIA
NARENDRA MODI	BARBADOS
LORD'S	NEW ZEALAND

CRICKET COLOURING #3

COLOUR IN THE IMAGE TO BRING IT TO LIFE

17

WHO AM I?

CAN YOU USE THESE CLUES TO FIGURE OUT WHO THE MYSTERY PLAYER IS? THEY COULD BE RETIRED OR STILL PLAYING

ANSWER ON PAGE: 86

1) I WAS BORN IN NEW ZEALAND BUT PLAY FOR ANOTHER COUNTRY.

2) I HAVE AN O.B.E.

3) I WAS IN THE 2019 WORLD CUP-WINNING SQUAD.

I AM:

_____

18

CRICKET FACT #5

DID YOU KNOW?

AUSTRALIA ARE CONSIDERED THE MOST SUCCESSFUL INTERNATIONAL CRICKET TEAM IN TERMS OF WORLD CUP AND TEST VICTORIES.

HISTORY

HOW MANY OF THESE QUIZ QUESTIONS CAN YOU GET RIGHT? THIS QUIZ IS ALL ABOUT THE HISTORY OF CRICKET

QUESTION 1:

WHAT COUNTRY DID CRICKET ORIGINATE IN?

QUESTION 2:

WHAT WERE THE FIRST CRICKET BALLS MADE OF?

QUESTION 3:

WHAT COUNTRY HOSTED THE FIRST CRICKET WORLD CUP?

QUESTION 4:

WHAT YEAR WAS THE FIRST EVER ASHES TEST SERIES PLAYED?

QUESTION 5:

IN 1844, THE FIRST EVER INTERNATIONAL CRICKET MATCH TOOK PLACE. CAN YOU GUESS WHAT TEAMS PLAYED IN THE GAME?

BEST BOWLERS

HOW MANY OF THESE BOWLERS CAN YOU FIND IN THE WORD SEARCH?

```
N D X P Y T P B K W F S B V N Q T
F I S G A W X S P H F Q B Q L G E
M O F M L O Z O B T A H O J J V V
M U R A L I T H A R A N K F N G D
D Z Q G I E A T C N K K Z N O H I
E I Q I L D F G P I J G K V R L Y
Z B I P L O F H O G L O I W P V U
H A Z L E W O O D N N G X W Y Z Y
S A Y V E A T I H G V Z M A M F R
T Y M C G R A T H A A C C R Q Y T
C U M M I N S T W R N L W I L N C
A B A N D E R S O N K X O H L U X
E S S I K O J O A E W T I W U W H
I T H H E H H M K R A B A D A Y K
L K W Z L V U F E Q P H E N X P J
E E I W A O D R S H E T B D G C D
N L N F H X Z P Y T B O R H N R U
```

ANDERSON	HAZLEWOOD	MURALITHARAN
ASHWIN	KHAN	RABADA
CUMMINS	LILLEE	WARNE
GARNER	MCGRATH	WOAKES

21

TEAM DESIGN

A NEW CRICKET TEAM HAS BEEN MADE BUT IT NEEDS YOUR HELP! CAN YOU DESIGN A KIT AND BADGE FOR THEM?

TEAM NAME:

_____

TEAM KIT

TEAM BADGE

CRICKET COLOURING #4

COLOUR IN THE IMAGE TO BRING IT TO LIFE

23

CRICKET FACT #6

DID YOU KNOW?

CRICKET BATS WERE ORIGINALLY CURVED, NOT STRAIGHT.

CODE CRACKING

USING THE TABLE BELOW CAN YOU DECODE THE NAMES OF
THESE CRICKET POSITIONS?

A	B	C	D	E	F	G	H	I	J	K	L	M	N	O	P	Q	R	S	T	U	V	W	X	Y	Z
Q	T	X	V	B	N	E	R	D	O	Z	C	P	H	L	G	U	I	F	K	A	S	Y	M	W	J

FUAQIB CBE

_____ ___

FCDG

____

PDV LNN

___ ___

XLSBI

_____

CRICKET SUBTRACTION

= 13   = 6   = 3

− = ___

− − 4 = ___

− 2 − 3 = ___

− − = ___

− 2 − = ___

26

BRAND ANAGRAMS

CAN YOU UNSCRAMBLE THESE ANAGRAMS TO WORK OUT WHICH POPULAR
CRICKET BRANDS SHOULD BE MADE UP OF THE LETTERS?

AKKARORBUO

YARG SCLOINL

---- -------

UNGN DAN OORME

---- --- -----

WEN BCALANE

--- -------

SOLUTION ON PAGE: 94

CRAZY MAZE #2

CAN YOU BOWL THE BALL THROUGH THE MAZE AND INTO THE STUMPS ON THE OTHER SIDE?

START

MAZE 2

END

CRICKET FACT #7

DID YOU KNOW?

CRICKET IS GENERALLY PLAYED IN THREE MAIN FORMATS: TWENTY20, ONE-DAY INTERNATIONALS AND TEST MATCHES.

BAT DESIGN

DESIGN THE FRONT AND BACK OF YOUR VERY OWN CRICKET
BAT. FEEL FREE TO EXPERIMENT WITH DIFFERENT COLOURS

FRONT   BACK

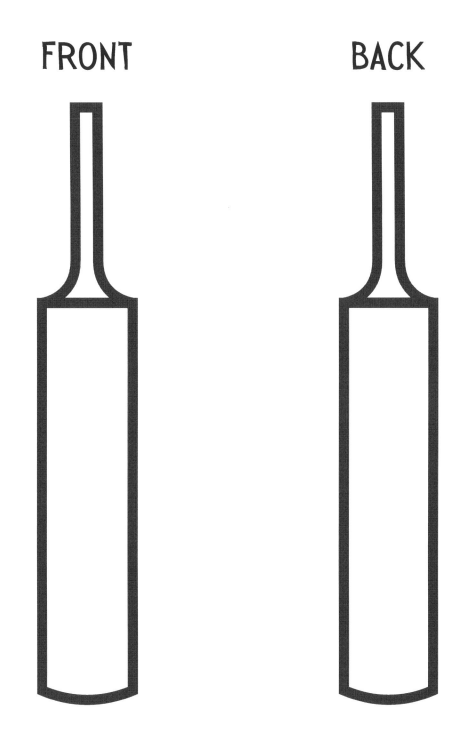

CRICKET COLOURING #5

COLOUR IN THE IMAGE TO BRING IT TO LIFE

THE WORLD CUP

HOW MANY OF THESE QUIZ QUESTIONS CAN YOU GET RIGHT? THIS QUIZ IS ALL ABOUT THE WORLD CUP

QUESTION 1:

WHAT YEAR WAS THE FIRST WORLD CUP HELD?

QUESTION 2:

BERMUDA AND IRELAND BOTH HAD THEIR FIRST WORLD CUP DEBUTS IN THE SAME YEAR. WHAT YEAR WAS THIS?

QUESTION 3:

WHICH TEAM HAS WON THE MOST WORLD CUPS?

QUESTION 4:

WHICH TEAM WON THE TOURNAMENT THREE TIMES IN A ROW, WINNING IN 1999, 2003 AND 2007?

QUESTION 5:

WHAT IS THE FORMAT OF WORLD CUP MATCHES? ARE THEY TWENTY20 GAMES, ONE-DAY INTERNATIONAL GAMES OR TEST MATCHES?

WHO AM I?

CAN YOU USE THESE CLUES TO FIGURE OUT WHO THE MYSTERY PLAYER IS? THEY COULD BE RETIRED OR STILL PLAYING

ANSWER ON PAGE: 87

1) I AM SAID TO HAVE BEEN ONE OF THE BEST TWENTY20 BATTERS.

2) I PLAYED FOR THE WEST INDIES.

3) I WAS THE FIRST PLAYER TO HIT A 6 IN THE FIRST BALL OF A TEST MATCH.

I AM:

_____

BADGE DESIGN

DESIGN A BADGE FOR YOUR CRICKET DREAM TEAM USING
DIFFERENT COLOURS AND PATTERNS

CRICKET FACT #8

DID YOU KNOW?

THE ASHES IS A TEST MATCH THAT HAPPENS EVERY TWO YEARS, EXCLUSIVELY BETWEEN ENGLAND AND AUSTRALIA.

PLAYER SPECIALITIES

CAN YOU JOIN UP THE PLAYER TO THEIR SPECIALITY?

SURESH RAINA	WICKET KEEPER
ADAM GILCHRIST	SEAM BOWLER
VIRAT KOHLI	FIELDER
JIMMY ANDERSON	SPIN BOWLER
SHANE WARNE	BATTER

CRICKET COLOURING #6

COLOUR IN THE IMAGE TO BRING IT TO LIFE

TEAM ANAGRAMS

CAN YOU UNSCRAMBLE THESE ANAGRAMS TO WORK OUT WHICH
INTERNATIONAL TEAM SHOULD BE MADE UP OF THE LETTERS?

IEBBAZWM

- - - - - - - -

STEW DSIEIN

- - - -   - - - - - -

SOHUT AAIFRC

- - - - -   - - - - - -

ATPKSIAN

- - - - - - - -

RATE A PLAYER #2

CHOOSE A CRICKET PLAYER AND RATE ALL OF THEIR SKILLS OUT OF 100.
WHAT AREAS OF THEIR GAME DO YOU THINK THEY COULD IMPROVE?

PLAYER NAME:

_____

BATTING: /100

BOWLING: /100

THROWING   /100

CATCHING: /100

FIELDING: /100

SPEED: /100

AGILITY: /100

CRICKET FACT #9

DID YOU KNOW?

A CRICKET GAME HAS TWO

UMPIRES ON THE FIELD AND

ONE OFF THE FIELD.

WORD SEARCH #3

ANSWERS ON PAGE: 95

INTERNATIONAL TEAMS

HOW MANY OF THESE INTERNATIONAL TEAMS CAN YOU FIND IN THE WORD SEARCH?

AUSTRALIA

BANGLADESH

CANADA

41 ENGLAND

INDIA

KENYA

NEW ZEALAND

PAKISTAN

SOUTH AFRICA

SRI LANKA

WEST INDIES

ZIMBABWE

CRICKET ADDITION

🏏 = 7   🪖 = 5   🏏 = 3

🏏 + 🪖 = ___

🏏 + 🏏 + 4 = ___

🏏 + 2 + 3 = ___

🏏 + 🪖 + 🏏 = ___

🪖 + 2 + 🏏 = ___

42

CODE CRACKING

USING THE TABLE BELOW CAN YOU DECODE THE NAMES OF
THESE CRICKET TOURNAMENTS?

A	B	C	D	E	F	G	H	I	J	K	L	M	N	O	P	Q	R	S	T	U	V	W	X	Y	Z
Q	T	X	V	B	N	E	R	D	O	Z	C	P	H	L	G	U	I	F	K	A	S	Y	M	W	J

QFRBF

_ _ _ _ _

HQKYBFK FBIDBF

_ _ _ _ _ _ _   _ _ _ _ _ _

DXX YLICV XAG

_ _ _   _ _ _ _ _   _ _ _

DHVDQH GIBPDBI CBQEAB

_ _ _ _ _ _   _ _ _ _ _ _   _ _ _ _ _ _

WHO AM I?

CAN YOU USE THESE CLUES TO FIGURE OUT WHO THE MYSTERY PLAYER IS? THEY COULD BE RETIRED OR STILL PLAYING

ANSWER ON PAGE: 88

1) I AM THE ONLY CRICKETER TO BE INVOLVED IN 100 TEST VICTORIES.

2) I CAPTAINED MY TEAM TO CONSECUTIVE WORLD CUP VICTORIES IN 2003 AND 2007.

3) I WAS BORN IN TASMANIA.

I AM:

_____

44

PLAYERS

HOW MANY OF THESE QUIZ QUESTIONS CAN YOU GET RIGHT? THIS QUIZ IS ALL ABOUT CRICKET PLAYERS

QUESTION 1:

MUTTIAH MURALITHARAN WAS ONE OF THE BEST BOWLERS. DID HE USED TO BOWL SPIN, SWING OR SEAM?

QUESTION 2:

SIR DON BRADMAN IS OFTEN REFERRED TO AS ONE OF THE GREATEST CRICKETERS OF ALL TIME. WHICH COUNTRY DID HE PLAY FOR?

QUESTION 3:

WHICH PLAYER HAD THE SHOT, 'THE SWITCH HIT', NAMED AFTER HIM?

QUESTION 4:

WHICH PLAYER IS COMMONLY KNOWN AS 'THE SLINGER' DUE TO HIS BOWLING TECHNIQUE?

QUESTION 5:

WHICH PLAYER CAPTAINED ENGLAND TO THEIR 2019 WORLD CUP VICTORY?

CRICKET FACT #10

DID YOU KNOW?

A CRICKET BALL WEIGHS EXACTLY 163 GRAMS.

WORLD CUP VICTORIES

CAN YOU JOIN UP THE YEAR TO THE TEAM WHICH WON THE WORLD CUP IN THAT YEAR?

1975	ENGLAND
1996	INDIA
2011	SRI LANKA
2015	WEST INDIES
2019	AUSTRALIA

CRICKET COLOURING #7

COLOUR IN THE IMAGE TO BRING IT TO LIFE

48

CRAZY MAZE #3

CAN YOU BOWL THE BALL THROUGH THE MAZE AND INTO THE STUMPS ON THE OTHER SIDE?

START

MAZE 3

49

END

PERFECT PLAYER #2

BUILD YOUR PERFECT PLAYER BY USING ELEMENTS OF ALL THE BEST CRICKET PLAYERS, BOTH PAST AND PRESENT, E.G. SAQLAIN MUSHTAQ'S RIGHT ARM

BATTING ABILITY: _____

LEFT ARM: _____

RIGHT ARM: _____

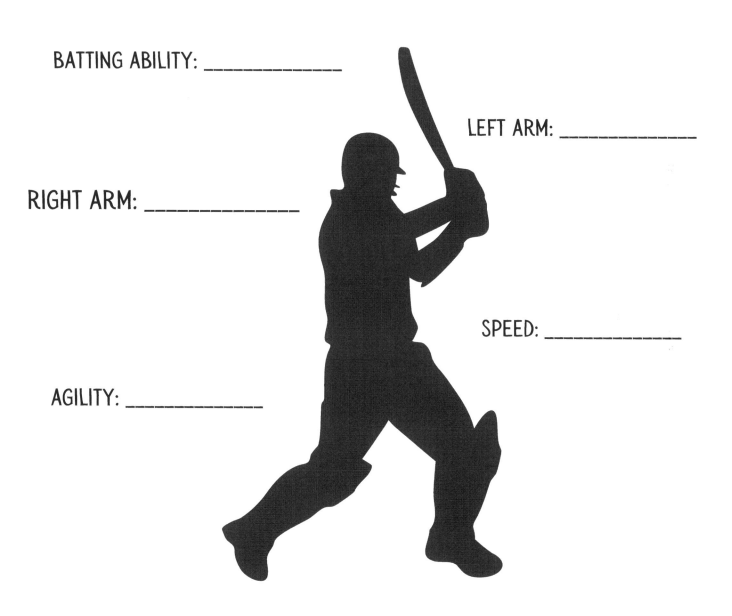

SPEED: _____

AGILITY: _____

CRICKET FACT #11

DID YOU KNOW?

THE FIRST EVER CRICKET WORLD CUP WAS HELD IN ENGLAND IN 1975.

POSITION ANAGRAMS

CAN YOU UNSCRAMBLE THESE ANAGRAMS TO WORK OUT WHICH POSITION
SHOULD BE MADE UP OF THE LETTERS?

LLGYU

_ _ _ _ _ _

IDM TWKICE

_ _ _   _ _ _ _ _ _

WEKIKREETPEC

_ _ _ _ _ _ _ _ _ _ _ _

THDIR ANM

_ _ _ _ _   _ _ _

TEAM DESIGN

A NEW CRICKET TEAM HAS BEEN MADE BUT IT NEEDS YOUR HELP! CAN YOU DESIGN A KIT AND BADGE FOR THEM?

TEAM NAME:

TEAM KIT

TEAM BADGE

CRICKET COLOURING #8

COLOUR IN THE IMAGE TO BRING IT TO LIFE

54

CRICKET FACT #12

DID YOU KNOW?

THERE ARE 11 PLAYERS ON EACH TEAM. WHILST IN PLAY, THERE WILL BE 11 FIELDERS PRESENT ON ONE TEAM AND 2 BATTERS PRESENT ON THE FIELD FOR THE OPPOSITION.

TECHNICAL KNOWLEDGE

HOW MANY OF THESE QUIZ QUESTIONS CAN YOU GET RIGHT? THIS QUIZ IS ALL ABOUT KNOWLEDGE OF THE GAME

QUESTION 1:

HOW MANY PLAYERS PLAY ON A CRICKET TEAM?

QUESTION 2:

WHAT IS THE POSITION CALLED FOR THE PLAYER WHO STANDS CLOSE TO THE WICKETKEEPER IN THE HOPE OF MAKING A CATCH?

QUESTION 3:

WHAT IS IT CALLED WHEN A BATSMAN SCORES 100 RUNS?

QUESTION 4:

HOW MANY RUNS ARE SCORED WHEN A BATTER HITS THE BALL PAST THE BOUNDARY, BUT IT TAKES A BOUNCE ON THE FIELD BEFORE THE BOUNDARY?

QUESTION 5:

WHAT DOES 'LBW' STAND FOR?

CODE CRACKING

USING THE TABLE BELOW CAN YOU DECODE THE NAMES OF THESE CRICKET STADIUMS?

A	B	C	D	E	F	G	H	I	J	K	L	M	N	O	P	Q	R	S	T	U	V	W	X	Y	Z
Q	T	X	V	B	N	E	R	D	O	Z	C	P	H	L	G	U	I	F	K	A	S	Y	M	W	J

BVBH EQIVBHF

_ _ _ _   _ _ _ _ _ _ _

QVBCQDVB LSQC

_ _ _ _ _ _ _   _ _ _ _ _

ILFB TLYC

_ _ _ _   _ _ _ _

QIAH OQDKCBW FKQVDAP

57   _ _ _ _   _ _ _ _ _ _ _   _ _ _ _ _ _

ENGLAND WINNERS

HOW MANY 2019 WORLD CUP WINNERS CAN YOU FIND IN THE WORD SEARCH?

```
O D Z W L X H J D U N L A J P L A
U Y U Q Z J F N S X D P T E K U Y
K D F Y J O A O S O I A S O P X N
P M T I R O T T J S A D U K P D Q
C L C Y L W A F B K K T B H U X N
A I U O R O L F R Q W M G W K M P
Q O R N B A I R S T O W W T I Z E
J P R P K K D R O Y O S L C J O Q
H Y A W V E S O R P D C E X M E W
C B N T M S T O M T V X H Y V S D
K S K Z U P S T O K E S H X P P L
P T B U T T L E R Y W H Q D B R F
T N C Y Z I N R G A I I C D S H Z
E D K I F G G M A P S D S V Y P R
V U B Y R E I A N U G H U G H G J
M B Q X D N S S M Y M A I N V H N
O B R N I B T Q U V D P B D L Z Y
```

ALI	MORGAN	ROY
BAIRSTOW	PLUNKETT	STOKES
BUTTLER	RASHID	WOAKES
CURRAN	ROOT	WOOD

58

CRICKET SUBTRACTION

🏏 = 20	⛑ = 11	✕ = 6

🏏 − ⛑ = ___

🏏 − ✕ − 4 = ___

✕ − 2 − 3 = ___

🏏 − ⛑ − ✕ = ___

⛑ − 2 − ✕ = ___

CRICKET FACT #13

DID YOU KNOW?

WEST INDIES BATSMAN BRIAN LARA HAS THE HIGHEST INDIVIDUAL SCORE IN TEST CRICKET, SCORING 400 NOT OUT IN 2004 VS ENGLAND.

TEAM MANAGERS

CAN YOU JOIN UP THE MANAGER TO THE TEAM WHICH THEY MANAGED?

JOHN BUCHANAN	ENGLAND
MIKE HESSON	BANGLADESH
TREVOR BAYLISS	AUSTRALIA
RAVI SHASTRI	NEW ZEALAND
DAV WHATMORE	INDIA

CRICKET COLOURING #9

COLOUR IN THE IMAGE TO BRING IT TO LIFE

62

WHO AM I?

CAN YOU USE THESE CLUES TO FIGURE OUT WHO THE MYSTERY PLAYER IS? THEY COULD BE RETIRED OR STILL PLAYING

ANSWER ON PAGE: 89

1) I HAVE CAPTAINED THE INDIA NATIONAL TEAM.

2) SOME OF MY NICKNAMES INCLUDE 'CHIKU' AND 'THE RUN MACHINE'.

3) I'M THE FASTEST BATSMAN TO SCORE 12,000 RUNS IN ONE DAY INTERNATIONAL CRICKET.

I AM:

_____

BADGE DESIGN

DESIGN A BADGE FOR YOUR CRICKET DREAM TEAM USING
DIFFERENT COLOURS AND PATTERNS

CRICKET FACT #14

DID YOU KNOW?

THE FIRST EVER RECORDED

GAME WAS PLAYED IN 1646.

SOLUTION ON PAGE: 94

CRAZY MAZE #4

CAN YOU BOWL THE BALL THROUGH THE MAZE AND INTO THE STUMPS
ON THE OTHER SIDE?

START

MAZE 4

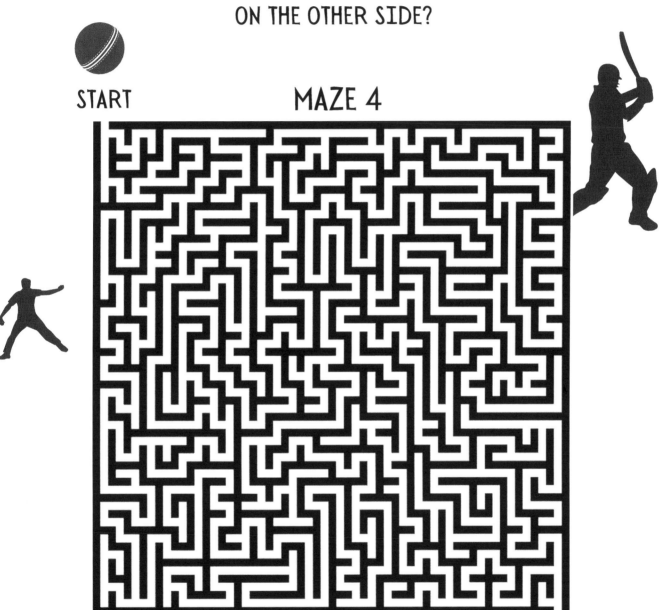

END

THE ASHES

HOW MANY OF THESE QUIZ QUESTIONS CAN YOU GET RIGHT? THIS QUIZ IS ALL ABOUT THE ASHES

QUESTION 1:

WHICH TWO TEAMS PLAY IN THE ASHES?

QUESTION 2:

THE ASHES URN (TROPHY) IS BELIEVED TO CONTAIN THE BURNED ASHES OF WHAT INSIDE?

QUESTION 3:

WHO WAS THE FIRST WINNER OF THE ASHES SERIES?

QUESTION 4:

HOW OFTEN IS THE ASHES TEST MATCH HELD?

QUESTION 5:

WHO WON THE 2021/22 ASHES?

CRICKET FACT #15

DID YOU KNOW?

CRICKET ORIGINATED IN
ENGLAND.

BAT DESIGN

DESIGN THE FRONT AND BACK OF YOUR VERY OWN CRICKET
BAT. FEEL FREE TO EXPERIMENT WITH DIFFERENT COLOURS

FRONT BACK

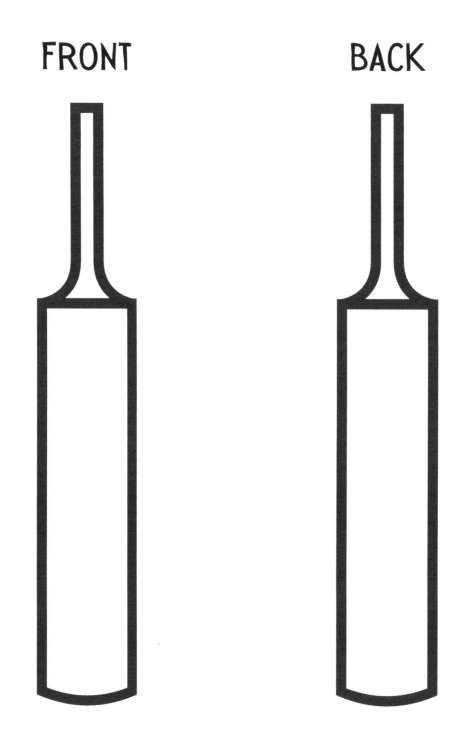

CRICKET COLOURING #10

COLOUR IN THE IMAGE TO BRING IT TO LIFE

70

ANSWER PAGES

PLAYER TEAMS

CAN YOU JOIN UP THE PLAYER TO THEIR INTERNATIONAL TEAM?

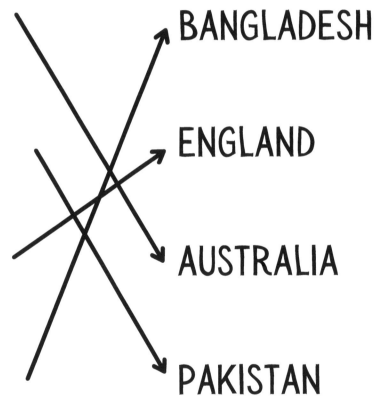

JOSH HAZLEWOOD — AUSTRALIA

BABAR AZAM — PAKISTAN

JOE ROOT — ENGLAND

SHAKIB AL HASAN — BANGLADESH

RAVINDRA JADEJA ⟶ INDIA

STADIUM LOCATIONS

CAN YOU JOIN UP THE STADIUM TO ITS LOCATION?

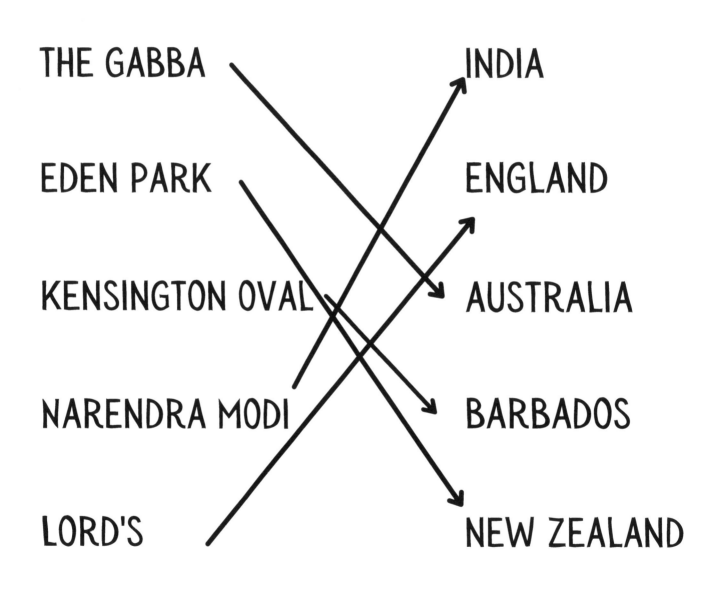

THE GABBA

EDEN PARK

KENSINGTON OVAL

NARENDRA MODI

LORD'S

INDIA

ENGLAND

AUSTRALIA

BARBADOS

NEW ZEALAND

PLAYER SPECIALITIES

CAN YOU JOIN UP THE PLAYER TO THEIR SPECIALITY?

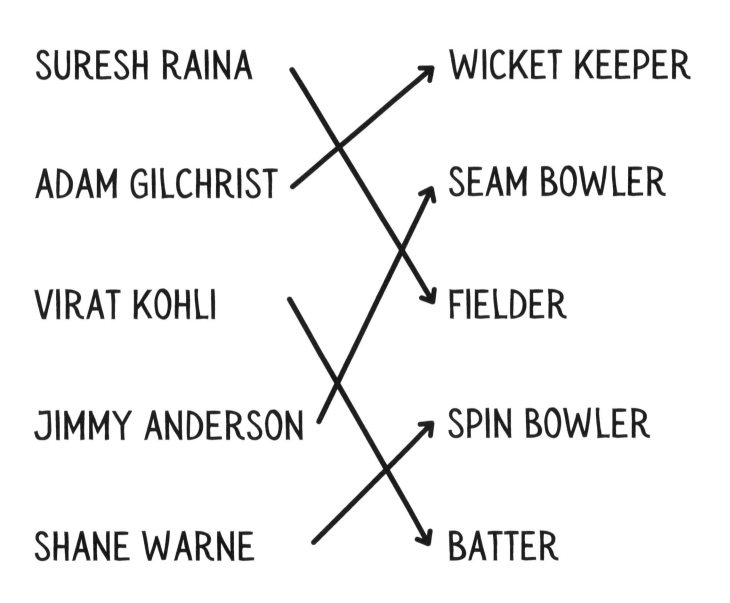

SURESH RAINA   WICKET KEEPER

ADAM GILCHRIST   SEAM BOWLER

VIRAT KOHLI   FIELDER

JIMMY ANDERSON   SPIN BOWLER

SHANE WARNE   BATTER

WORLD CUP VICTORIES

CAN YOU JOIN UP THE YEAR TO THE TEAM WHICH WON THE WORLD CUP IN THAT YEAR?

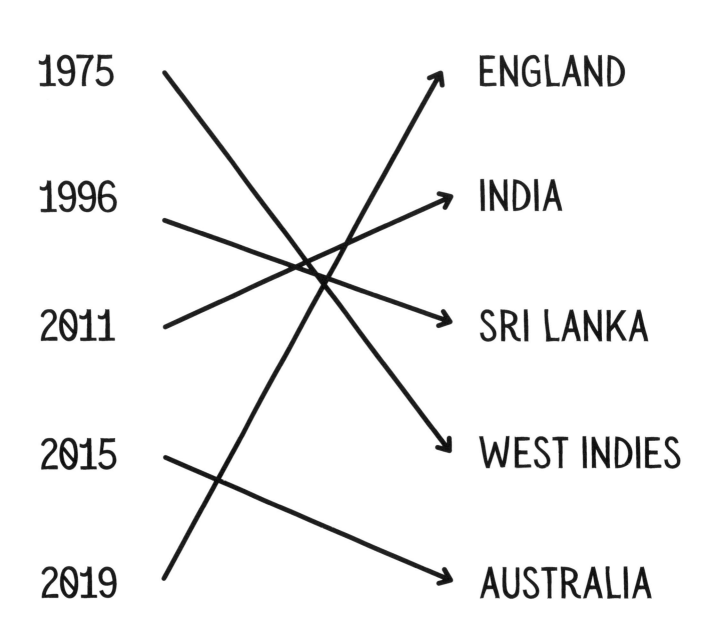

1975

1996

2011

2015

2019

ENGLAND

INDIA

SRI LANKA

WEST INDIES

AUSTRALIA

TEAM MANAGERS

CAN YOU JOIN UP THE MANAGER TO THE TEAM WHICH THEY MANAGED?

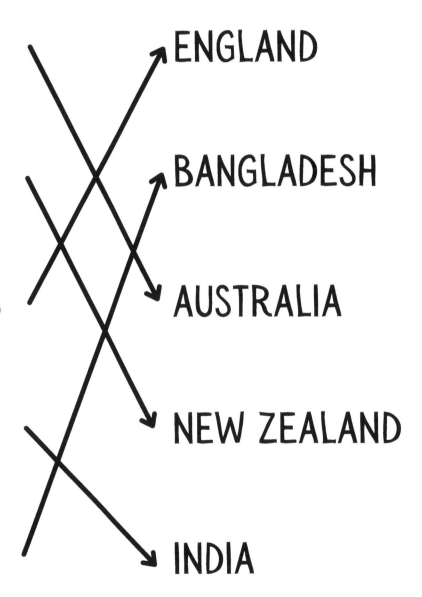

JOHN BUCHANAN — AUSTRALIA

MIKE HESSON — NEW ZEALAND

TREVOR BAYLISS — ENGLAND

RAVI SHASTRI — INDIA

DAV WHATMORE — BANGLADESH

PLAYER ANAGRAMS

CAN YOU UNSCRAMBLE THESE ANAGRAMS TO WORK OUT WHICH PLAYER SHOULD BE MADE UP OF THE LETTERS?

FEEDDIR OFLINFFT

FREDDIE FLINTOFF

RIYCK GTONINP

RICKY PONTING

NMIAR AHKN

IMRAN KHAN

KENVI EEPRINSTE

KEVIN PIETERSEN

BRAND ANAGRAMS

CAN YOU UNSCRAMBLE THESE ANAGRAMS TO WORK OUT WHICH POPULAR
CRICKET BRANDS SHOULD BE MADE UP OF THE LETTERS?

AKKARORBUO

KOOKABURRA

YARG SCLOINL

GRAY NICOLLS

UNGN DAN OORME

GUNN AND MOORE

WEN BCALANE

NEW BALANCE

TEAM ANAGRAMS

CAN YOU UNSCRAMBLE THESE ANAGRAMS TO WORK OUT WHICH WORLD CUP TEAM SHOULD BE MADE UP OF THE LETTERS?

IEBBAZWM
ZIMBABWE

STEW DSIEIN
WEST INDIES

SOHUT AAIFRC
SOUTH AFRICA

ATPKSIAN
PAKISTAN

POSITION ANAGRAMS

CAN YOU UNSCRAMBLE THESE ANAGRAMS TO WORK OUT WHICH POSITION
SHOULD BE MADE UP OF THE LETTERS?

LLGYU

GULLY

IDM TWKICE

MID WICKET

WEKIKREETPEC

WICKETKEEPER

THDIR ANM

THIRD MAN

HISTORY

HOW MANY OF THESE QUIZ QUESTIONS CAN YOU GET RIGHT? THIS QUIZ IS ALL ABOUT THE HISTORY OF CRICKET

QUESTION 1:

WHAT COUNTRY DID CRICKET ORIGINATE IN?

ENGLAND

QUESTION 2:

WHAT WERE THE FIRST CRICKET BALLS MADE OF?

WOOL

QUESTION 3:

WHAT COUNTRY HOSTED THE FIRST CRICKET WORLD CUP?

ENGLAND

QUESTION 4:

WHAT YEAR WAS THE FIRST EVER ASHES TEST SERIES PLAYED?

1882

QUESTION 5:

IN 1844, THE FIRST EVER INTERNATIONAL CRICKET MATCH TOOK PLACE. CAN YOU GUESS WHAT TEAMS PLAYED IN THE GAME?

UNITED STATES VS CANADA

81

THE WORLD CUP

HOW MANY OF THESE QUIZ QUESTIONS CAN YOU GET RIGHT? THIS QUIZ IS ALL ABOUT THE WORLD CUP

QUESTION 1:

WHAT YEAR WAS THE FIRST WORLD CUP HELD?

1975

QUESTION 2:

BERMUDA AND IRELAND BOTH HAD THEIR FIRST WORLD CUP DEBUTS IN THE SAME YEAR. WHAT YEAR WAS THIS?

2007

QUESTION 3:

WHICH TEAM HAS WON MOST WORLD CUPS?

AUSTRALIA

QUESTION 4:

WHICH TEAM WON THE TOURNAMENT THREE TIMES IN A ROW, WINNING IN 1999, 2003 AND 2007?

AUSTRALIA

QUESTION 5:

WHAT IS THE FORMAT OF WORLD CUP MATCHES? ARE THEY TWENTY20 GAMES, ONE-DAY INTERNATIONAL GAMES OR TEST MATCHES?

ONE-DAY INTERNATIONAL GAMES

PLAYERS

HOW MANY OF THESE QUIZ QUESTIONS CAN YOU GET RIGHT? THIS QUIZ IS ALL ABOUT CRICKET PLAYERS

QUESTION 1:

MUTTIAH MURALITHARAN WAS ONE OF THE BEST BOWLERS. DID HE USED TO BOWL SPIN, SWING OR SEAM?

SPIN

QUESTION 2:

SIR DON BRADMAN IS OFTEN REFERRED TO AS ONE OF THE GREATEST CRICKETERS OF ALL TIME. WHICH COUNTRY DID HE PLAY FOR?

AUSTRALIA

QUESTION 3:

WHICH PLAYER HAD THE SHOT, 'THE SWITCH HIT', NAMED AFTER HIM?

KEVIN PIETERSEN

QUESTION 4:

WHICH PLAYER IS COMMONLY KNOWN AS 'THE SLINGER' DUE TO HIS BOWLING TECHNIQUE?

LASITH MALINGA

QUESTION 5:

WHICH PLAYER CAPTAINED ENGLAND TO THEIR 2019 WORLD CUP VICTORY?

EOIN MORGAN

TECHNICAL KNOWLEDGE

HOW MANY OF THESE QUIZ QUESTIONS CAN YOU GET RIGHT? THIS QUIZ IS ALL ABOUT KNOWLEDGE OF THE GAME

QUESTION 1:

HOW MANY PLAYERS PLAY ON A CRICKET TEAM?

11

QUESTION 2:

WHAT IS THE POSITION CALLED FOR THE PLAYER WHO STANDS CLOSE TO THE WICKETKEEPER IN THE HOPE OF MAKING A CATCH?

SLIP

QUESTION 3:

WHAT IS IT CALLED WHEN A BATSMAN SCORES 100 RUNS?

CENTURY

QUESTION 4:

HOW MANY RUNS ARE SCORED WHEN A BATTER HITS THE BALL PAST THE BOUNDARY, BUT IT TAKES A BOUNCE ON THE FIELD BEFORE THE BOUNDARY?

4

QUESTION 5:

WHAT DOES 'LBW' STAND FOR?

LEG BEFORE WICKET

THE ASHES

HOW MANY OF THESE QUIZ QUESTIONS CAN YOU GET RIGHT? THIS QUIZ IS ALL ABOUT THE ASHES

QUESTION 1:

WHICH TWO TEAMS PLAY IN THE ASHES?

ENGLAND AND AUSTRALIA

QUESTION 2:

THE ASHES URN (TROPHY) IS BELIEVED TO CONTAIN THE BURNED ASHES OF WHAT INSIDE?

CRICKET BALL

QUESTION 3:

WHO WAS THE FIRST WINNER OF THE ASHES SERIES?

ENGLAND

QUESTION 4:

HOW OFTEN IS THE ASHES TEST MATCH HELD?

EVERY TWO YEARS

QUESTION 5:

WHO WON THE 2021/22 ASHES?

AUSTRALIA

WHO AM I?

CAN YOU USE THESE CLUES TO FIGURE OUT WHO THE MYSTERY PLAYER IS? THEY COULD BE RETIRED OR STILL PLAYING

ANSWER ON PAGE

1) I WAS BORN IN NEW ZEALAND BUT PLAY FOR ANOTHER COUNTRY.

2) I HAVE AN O.B.E.

3) I WAS IN THE 2019 WORLD CUP-WINNING SQUAD.

I AM:
BEN STOKES

WHO AM I?

CAN YOU USE THESE CLUES TO FIGURE OUT WHO THE MYSTERY PLAYER IS? THEY COULD BE RETIRED OR STILL PLAYING

ANSWER ON PAGE

1) I AM SAID TO HAVE BEEN ONE OF THE BEST TWENTY20 BATTERS.

2) I PLAYED FOR THE WEST INDIES.

3) I WAS THE FIRST PLAYER TO HIT A 6 IN THE FIRST BALL OF A TEST MATCH.

I AM:
CHRIS GAYLE

WHO AM I?

CAN YOU USE THESE CLUES TO FIGURE OUT WHO THE MYSTERY PLAYER IS? THEY COULD BE RETIRED OR STILL PLAYING

ANSWER ON PAGE

1) I AM THE ONLY CRICKETER TO BE INVOLVED IN 100 TEST VICTORIES.

2) I CAPTAINED MY TEAM TO CONSECUTIVE WORLD CUP VICTORIES IN 2003 AND 2007.

3) I WAS BORN IN TASMANIA.

I AM:
RICKY PONTING

WHO AM I?

CAN YOU USE THESE CLUES TO FIGURE OUT WHO THE MYSTERY PLAYER IS? THEY COULD BE RETIRED OR STILL PLAYING

ANSWER ON PAGE

1) I HAVE CAPTAINED THE INDIA NATIONAL TEAM.

2) SOME OF MY NICKNAMES INCLUDE 'CHIKU' AND 'THE RUN MACHINE'.

3) I'M THE FASTEST BATSMAN TO SCORE 12,000 RUNS IN ONE DAY INTERNATIONAL CRICKET.

I AM:

VIRAT KOHLI

🔒 CODE CRACKING 🔒

USING THE TABLE BELOW CAN YOU DECODE THE NAMES OF
THESE 2019 WORLD CUP CRICKET TEAMS?

A	B	C	D	E	F	G	H	I	J	K	L	M	N	O	P	Q	R	S	T	U	V	W	X	Y	Z
Q	T	X	V	B	N	E	R	D	O	Z	C	P	H	L	G	U	I	F	K	A	S	Y	M	W	J

FLAKR QNIDXQ

SOUTH AFRICA

QNERQHDFKQH

AFGHANISTAN

YBFK DHVDBF

WEST INDIES

QAFKIQCDQ

AUSTRALIA

90

 CODE CRACKING

USING THE TABLE BELOW CAN YOU DECODE THE NAMES OF
THESE CRICKET POSITIONS?

A	B	C	D	E	F	G	H	I	J	K	L	M	N	O	P	Q	R	S	T	U	V	W	X	Y	Z
Q	T	X	V	B	N	E	R	D	O	Z	C	P	H	L	G	U	I	F	K	A	S	Y	M	W	J

FUAQIB CBE

SQUARE LEG

FCDG

SLIP

PDV LNN

MID OFF

XLSBI

COVER

91

CODE CRACKING

USING THE TABLE BELOW CAN YOU DECODE THE NAMES OF
THESE CRICKET TOURNAMENTS?

A	B	C	D	E	F	G	H	I	J	K	L	M	N	O	P	Q	R	S	T	U	V	W	X	Y	Z
Q	T	X	V	B	N	E	R	D	O	Z	C	P	H	L	G	U	I	F	K	A	S	Y	M	W	J

QFRBF

ASHES

HQKYBFK FBIDBF

NATWEST SERIES

DXX YLICV XAG

ICC WORLD CUP

DHVDQH GIBPDBI CBQEAB

INDIAN PREMIER LEAGUE

92

CODE CRACKING

USING THE TABLE BELOW CAN YOU DECODE THE NAMES OF
THESE CRICKET STADIUMS?

A	B	C	D	E	F	G	H	I	J	K	L	M	N	O	P	Q	R	S	T	U	V	W	X	Y	Z
Q	T	X	V	B	N	E	R	D	O	Z	C	P	H	L	G	U	I	F	K	A	S	Y	M	W	J

BVBH EQIVBHF

EDEN GARDENS

QVBCQDVB LSQC

ADELAIDE OVAL

ILFB TLYC

ROSE BOWL

QIAH OQDKCBW FKQVDAP

ARUN JAITLEY STADIUM

CRAZY MAZE

ANSWER PAGE

MAZE 1

MAZE 2

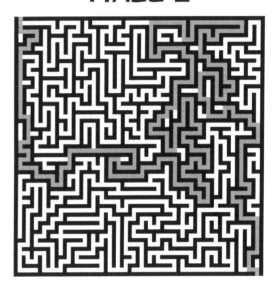

MAZE 3

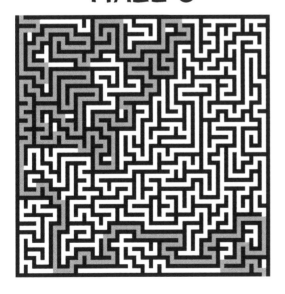

MAZE 4

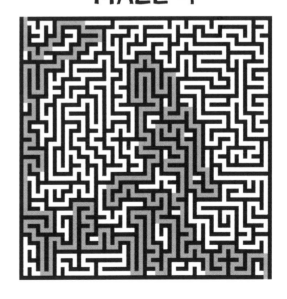

WORD SEARCHES
ANSWER PAGE

BEST BATSMEN

BEST BOWLERS

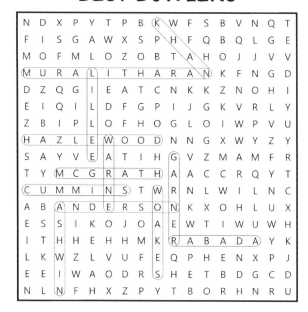

INTERNATIONAL TEAMS

WORLD CUP WINNERS

CRICKET ADDITION

= 5   = 4   = 2

+ = ___9___

+ + 4 = ___11___

+ 2 + 3 = ___7___

+ + = ___11___

+ 2 + = ___8___

CRICKET SUBTRACTION

$$\text{(ball)} = 13 \quad \text{(helmet)} = 6 \quad \text{(stumps)} = 3$$

$$\text{(ball)} - \text{(helmet)} = \quad \underline{7}$$

$$\text{(ball)} - \text{(stumps)} - 4 = \quad \underline{6}$$

$$\text{(helmet)} - 2 - 3 = \quad \underline{1}$$

$$\text{(ball)} - \text{(helmet)} - \text{(stumps)} = \quad \underline{4}$$

$$\text{(helmet)} - 2 - \text{(stumps)} = \quad \underline{1}$$

CRICKET ADDITION

$$\text{(ball)} = 7 \quad \text{(helmet)} = 5 \quad \text{(bats)} = 3$$

$\text{(ball)} + \text{(helmet)} = \quad\quad \underline{12}$

$\text{(ball)} + \text{(bats)} + 4 = \quad\quad \underline{14}$

$\text{(bats)} + 2 + 3 = \quad\quad \underline{8}$

$\text{(ball)} + \text{(helmet)} + \text{(bats)} = \quad\quad \underline{15}$

$\text{(helmet)} + 2 + \text{(bats)} = \quad\quad \underline{10}$

98

CRICKET SUBTRACTION

= 20   = 11   = 6

− =   9

− − 4 =   10

− 2 − 3 =   1

− − =   3

− 2 − =   3

Printed in Great Britain
by Amazon

13899539R00059